WINNING
THE INNER GAME OF SALES

The Foundation of Success is Mindset

JOHN G. LESTER
ATTITUDE SELLING
MOUNTAIN LAKES, NEW JERSEY, USA

Copyright © 2022
JOHN G. LESTER
WINNING THE INNER GAME OF SALES
The Foundation of Success is Mindset
All rights reserved.

No part of this publication may be reproduced, distributed, or transmitted in any form or by any means, including photocopying, recording, or other electronic or mechanical methods, without the prior written permission of the publisher, except in the case of brief quotations embodied in critical reviews and certain other non-commercial uses permitted by copyright law.

JOHN G. LESTER

Printed in the United States of America
First Printing 2022
First Edition 2022

10 9 8 7 6 5 4 3 2 1

For permission requests, write to the publisher, addressed "Attention: Permissions Coordinator," at the address below.

Attitude Selling LLC
125 Boulevard
Mountain Lakes, NJ 07046
www.AttitudeSelling.com

Ordering Information:
Quantity sales. Special discounts are available on quantity purchases by corporations, associations, and others.
For details, contact the "Special Sales Department" at the address above.

Table of Contents

FOREWORD 1
INTRODUCTION 5
CHAPTER ONE 9
   The State of the Sales Business
CHAPTER TWO 17
   The Current Approaches Have Shortcomings
CHAPTER THREE 25
   The Impact to YOU
CHAPTER FOUR 33
   Introducing YOU
CHAPTER FIVE 41
   Understanding Your Market
CHAPTER SIX 49
   What YOU Bring to the Table
CHAPTER SEVEN 57
   Game Changing Perspectives
CHAPTER EIGHT 63
   Caring Counts
CHAPTER NINE 71
   You'll Walk Like a Superhero
CHAPTER TEN 79
   Expense Paid Vacations in Hawaii Aren't Too Shabby
CONCLUSION 85
A FEW WORDS 89
   On the Power of a Master Mind Group
NEXT STEPS 95
ACKNOWLEDGEMENTS 97
ABOUT THE AUTHOR 99

FOREWORD

"I'll check it out but if I can't get a Ferrari out of it, it's not worth my time."

I wish all of us had at least one friend who regularly makes statements that are completely natural, unpretentious, and effortless to them, but which clearly remind you of the difference in the level you're playing at.

For me, that is John Lester.

The Ferrari thing was something John said about a potential CEO he was considering working with to improve their company's sales process. For someone who comes from a world where the top salespeople wear Armani suits, get limousine service to-and-from hotels, and often make several times more money than their CEO, there's nothing extraordinary about it, and they have nobody to impress.

For me, a fledgling entrepreneur at the time, it set off sirens in my brain. It made me feel small, but more than that I felt guilty. Because the world John comes from is the exact same world you and I live in, and that success is available for the taking, no matter what you were told growing up. In our mind, we put arbitrary glass walls between the successful and ourselves. If you can't visualize collecting a $150,000 commission from a sale you made without your stomach coiling, you probably never will.

That's just the first of many lessons I learned from John, as you will too from this book. A lot of sales books focus on the "tactics" — what to say when, how to negotiate, how to this, how to that. But most of them miss the point. This book focuses on what's beneath the iceberg — expectations, strategy, confidence, and other critical things.

John often gives me the impression of an old military general who's been through several wars and has survived multiple attempts on his life. He started his sales career in the late 70s, even briefly competing with the sales force of IBM during their golden years. He's seen so many deals miraculously succeed, so many companies miraculously disintegrate, and navigated the internal chaos associated with both, that he's a hardcore realist. A bloody tough weed, he talks straight, doesn't like roundabout answers to his questions, and doesn't take anyone's words at face value (especially those of his mentees and clients). I often squirm while discussing my business with him, because he'll unintentionally grind you like a defense lawyer until you confess to every crime you've committed and every lie you've told yourself that's holding back your success in sales.

He's also the guy you can always trust to have your back, and whose heart of gold just keeps on giving. If you read and think about the lessons in this book, I assure you that you will see your profession in a different light.

And who knows, one day your Ferrari might pass by his on the freeway.

Aman Y. Agarwal

Founder and CEO | Sanpram Transnational Corp

INTRODUCTION

"You're playing and you think everything is going fine. Then one thing goes wrong. And then another. And another. You try to fight back, but the harder you fight, the deeper you sink. Until you can't move... you can't breathe... because you're in over your head. Like quicksand."

- KEANU REEVES as Shane Falco in "The Replacements"

Sales can be a very difficult profession. It can also make your dreams come true.

But selling isn't simply a job. It's a Mindset and it's a mind game. The game, however, is with yourself more than its with the prospect or customer.

Consider, if you will, some statistics that speak to the current environment of sales.

Average sales turnover is 35 percent, higher than the average for all other industries at 13 percent. HubSpot reports that sales turnover is nearly three times higher than any other industry. SiriusDecisions data also shows that almost half (45 percent) of B2B sales organizations have turnover rates above 30 percent.

According to the [CSO Insights 2015 Sales Compensation and Performance Management Study](), only 54.6 percent of sales professionals produce enough revenue to meet quota.

In response to the question, "What is the number one reason salespeople miss their quota?" the following were offered as explanations:

- Not enough qualified leads
- Lack of sales training
- No formal sales process in place
- Managers can't effectively coach reps
- Ramping up reps is too slow
- Lost opportunities to no decision
- Competition beating us on price
- Sales burdened with administrative tasks
- Sales team not properly led
- Reps assigned unrealistic quotes
- Deals not closed, but still in pipeline
- Salespeople not properly hired

The interesting aspect of the above statistics is that there is no consideration for the most significant underlying cause of the lack of quota performance – salesperson Mindset.

If you successfully realign aspects of your Mindset, there is a very good chance you will achieve quota, and much more.

INTRODUCTION

Close your eyes, take a deep breath, and ask yourself, "What would my life look like if I were in the Achievers Circle?". Stay in that state and image how your family's daily existence would change for the better.

What about that vacation you have been dreaming of? The whole family relaxing in the sun.

The new car, the college tuition for the kids, helping your parents, saving for retirement, etc. All those aspirations you've been holding in your "someday I'll …" part of your brain.

How would my job or career be different? Be better?

The truth is very simple but difficult at the same time. When you're confident in yourself, when you're certain of your path and process, you generate an assurance that's transformative to yourself and to those with whom you come into contact. Very cool stuff.

Then all the other sales improvement methodologies have a chance to become effective for you. Then the sales training can actually work.

Or do you want to stay where you are. Are you comfortable not achieving your quota or your life goals? Do you enjoy saying "No" to your family? Do you need the waking up at night in a cold sweat because you're not sure if you'll have a job next week? The list goes on. You know it better than anyone else. You're living it.

So, the choice is yours. Spend the next 60 minutes reading this book. I guarantee that you will walk away with at least one attitude shifting idea.

"Victorious warriors win first and then go to war, while defeated warriors go to war first and then seek to win"

— **Sun Tzu, The Art of War**

CHAPTER ONE

The State of the Sales Business

Let's spend a few minutes and highlight some realities of being a professional salesperson. Don't be disillusioned by these. Rather, appreciate the nuances of the challenge in front of you in becoming a Sales Achiever.

Some Realities

These are taken from a number of sources. They may or may not be the most current but are useful to view as directional.

- At least half of all your prospects are bad fits for your offering
- 61% of salespeople consider selling harder or much harder than just five years ago
- Less than 20% of sales reps consistently ask for referrals
- According to one source, less than 25% of salespeople exceeded their quota last year.

Unwillingness to train new people

A simple fact of business is that it costs money to train people. Companies do not always see a return on that investment. Thus, more organizations over the years have reduced or eliminated their programs of hiring and fully training new sales reps.

- How companies react to low sales
- Depending on whose perspective you hear, there are multiple reason for organizations not achieving their quotas. The "usual suspects" include the market, the economy, the buyer, competition, price, product shortcomings, and of course, the salespeople.
- Everybody thinks that if they make a sale they know how to sell.
- And they're happy to tell you. Getting agreement from a few isolated individuals to try and/or buy your offering does not require the same skill set and disciplines needed to spend every day selling. Especially against a quota with a product / service you have no ability to impact.
- Selling is a long game. It is a process that requires an emotional ability more so than a technical one. Selling is mostly rejection.
- There is no accepted certification
- Many professions have certification bodies and ways to measure competence. The Accounting profession has, amongst others, the AICPA Certificate, the CPA designation, CFA, CFE, CIA, CMA, CGMA, EA, and CFSA. These are credentials that accounting professionals use

to enhance their careers and grow their skill. As well as potential employers to assess the value of the candidate.
- Similarly, doctors, financial advisors, mechanics, computer programmers, statisticians, real estate agents and brokers, and more have their own regulatory, licensing, certification, and continuing education standards.
- Interestingly, there is no such structure for sales professionals. There are for the product knowledge side of some of their roles, but not for the people-understanding and pure sales aspects.
- Most sales training may be outdated.
- That's not to say there isn't a tremendous amount of value in their thoughts and curricula. But be aware of the possible perspectives and limitations that might not reflect your current reality or play to your strengths. These programs also typically focus on the process of convincing and closing the buyer
- Let me repeat myself. There is value in many of these systems but more value in those based on recent research.
  o Dale Carnegie started over 100 years ago
  o Sandler – started in the late 1960's
  o Tom Hopkins – since 1976
  o "Spin Selling" was published in 1988
  o Chet Holmes "The Ultimate Sales Machine" was first published in the US in 2007
  o Jim Holden's "Power Base Selling" was released in 1990

- Many aspects of the sales process have been transferred to digital / automated leaving the more complex and human issues-oriented tasks to the salesperson.

"Today stretches ahead of you waiting to be shaped. You are the sculptor who gets to do the shaping. What today will be like is up to you."

Steve Maraboli

What the buyers think of you.

Take a deep breath and digest the following points:

A Harvard Business Review article, "7 Reasons Salespeople Don't Close the Deal" states

"According to a new study of more than 230 buyers, 12% of salespeople are excellent, 23% good, 38% average, and 27% poor.

The bad news is that the underperforming salespeople lack the self-awareness to know that buyers don't value them, nor do they understand why. They don't take the time to figure out why they lost a deal or longtime client. They either don't know why they weren't selected, or they reflexively blame it on factors out of their control."

The article continues by highlighting the 7 reasons why salespeople lose business:

- They are not trusted or respected
- They can't converse effectively with the senior executives
- They can't clearly explain how their solution helps the buyer's business
- They are too self-centered

- They use the wrong closing strategy
- They don't alleviate the risk of buying their solution
- They can't establish a personal connection with the buyer

And from a SuperOffice blog:

"Today's buyers prefer to conduct research and select what to buy on their own, without any influence from a vendor:

- Only 29% of buyers want to talk to a salesperson to learn more about a product,
- 57% of buyer decisions are made before buyers even pick up a phone to speak to a supplier,
- And, 34% of salespeople admit that closing deals is getting harder.

Surprisingly, only 17% of the entire B2B buying process is spent meeting with potential suppliers."

The buyers today are more aware of your company's products, services, and reputation than at any other time in selling history. They are also aware of the research on salespeople (your) behaviors. Such as that 80% of sales require five follow-ups after the initial contact, but 44% of salespeople give up after one.

Given then that buyers distrust and have a negative view of sellers, are more aware, can conduct most of their research online, and know that the majority of salespeople are less than professional – why should they want to speak and/or meet with you?

> *"Customers don't care at all whether you close the deal or not. They care about improving their business."*
>
> *– Aaron Ross*

Your Sales Manager

Your quota, leads, territory, working conditions, support, tension and more could, and most times do, depend upon your sales manager!

According to a Hubspot blog, here are some sobering metrics you should be aware of that your sales manager lives with and thus impact you:

- Sales managers cannot control 83% of the metrics they're held accountable to
- A full two-thirds of all salespeople miss quota
- Over half of all salespeople close at less than 40%
- 40% of salespeople can't understand customer pain
- Only 46% of reps feel their pipeline is accurate
- Almost half of all sales teams don't have a playbook
- Only 52% of salespeople can access key players

Here's an informative bit from Selling Power magazine about a top sales rep that was promoted to sales manager, "(he) was promoted to his position based on his sales ability and sales performance—but he didn't have a clue about managing a sales team. He held reps accountable for increasing sales and increasing sales performance, but he didn't communicate expectations. He managed by intimidation and not motivation—locking himself in his office and immersing himself in administrative tasks."

Unfortunately, this is not uncommon. The chance of you're working for a manager such as this is realistic. How much guidance and support you will receive from your sales manager is an open question.

Thus, the world of professional sales is not easy. Know that immediately and understand the ramifications. The simple truth is that success is up to YOU, and no one else. Keep reading and we'll show you more concerns!

> *The first thing the reasonable man must do is to be content with a very little knowledge and a very great deal of ignorance. The second thing he must do is to make the utmost possible use of the knowledge he has and not waste his energy crying for the moon. The third thing he must do is try and see clearly where his knowledge ends and his ignorance begins.*
>
> ***Arthur David Ritchie***

CHAPTER TWO

The Current Approaches Have Shortcomings

Sales is arguably the oldest profession. But techniques, knowledge, practices and buyers change. Much of what you will experience, or be asked to follow, is based on outdated concepts and attitudes.

Companies want their salespeople to be product experts

All too often hiring organizations will put their newly hired salespeople through an orientation and sales training session. Most of the time will be spent on two topics: navigating the organization internally and product training. They will spend vast amounts of time teaching the salespeople how the product works why its features are better than the competition and, in many cases, how to do a good demo of those product features.

This is not to say that understanding your product isn't important.

Let me provide an example. Imagine yourself going into a car dealership to purchase a new car. The salesperson approaches from across the room smiling broadly and greet you with a warm handshake and a "Welcome to our dealership". The salesperson then proceeds to explain to you in detail all of the car's features including the chassis, the suspension, the electrical wiring, the braking system the engine management system, the air conditioning recovery components, etc.

Are these important? Yes, of course. But you came in to purchase a vehicle that will allow you to transport your three children to their three different social and sports engagements, on the daily basis. Your concerns were around safety, seating capacity, gas mileage, resale value, and whether or not the seats and floor carpet shed stains.

Yes, product information is important. However, its real value is in helping the salesperson determine what problems to pursue and how they might be solved.

In his book "Selling to the C-Suite", Steven Bistritz shared research he had done over 10 years showing the decision-making criteria of executives. In as much as the percentages changed slightly during the course of the 10-year study, the top criteria from the perspective of the executives on with whom they would do business were relatively consistent. The top four concerns were:

- Ability to marshal resources
- Understand my business goals
- Responsiveness to my requests
- Willingness to be held accountable

In the 5th and the 10th year of the study the 'Ability to Marshall Resources' dropped below 'Knowledge of their own industry'. What was quite interesting about this study was that 'Knowledge of the

Company's Products' stayed below the other four or five mentioned criteria

The majority of the other criteria interestingly enough had to do with the ability of the selling individual and their company to become a part of the buyers' organization and Mindset

The prospect wants to buy a solution. But only to their problem, not your definition of it.

There is a term used to define the process of salespeople that begin a prospect meeting with an exhaustive telling of product feature, much like our car salesperson above. It is not so affectionately called "show up and throw up".

The fields of failed companies are littered with products and services that either did not have customer or market input or were never explained with the buyer's needs in mind. And that doesn't mean they were bad products!

Sales training is sporadic and focuses on process

One day, three days, one week - and no more. A good part of sales training is on process and language.

Sales training is treated like a silver bullet in many organizations. Management or sales management believes that by bringing in a sales training expert they can solve all of their low revenue issues.

Let's first clarify and agree that sales training has a definite place in helping salespeople and organizations increase their revenue, reduce their time to close, and increase their customer satisfaction. But it's not a silver bullet.

Most training programs make the assumption that the salesperson has resolved all of the questions in their mind and have resolved all of their Mindset issues. It focuses on the interaction with the prospect and or the customer. More recent sales trainings are designed to help the salesperson understand the Mindset of the buyer.

That being said, the real objective of any training is to modify behavior. Depending upon the 'expert', behavior modification or developing new habits can take 30 days, or 66 days, or – add whatever number works for you. But I haven't seen any research that says you can make significant and lasting change in 1 or 3 days – or a week.

Unfortunately, too often sales training is conducted over a single day or a few days. Hardly enough time for lasting change.

A few stats to reinforce the notion:

- The Association for Talent Development states that "up to 80% of new skills are lost within 1 week of training if the skills are not used".
- Up to 85% of sales training fails to deliver a positive ROI, according to the Chally Group.
- In a Xerox study, 87% of new skills are lost within a month of training.

One of the common aspects of sales training is to provide the sales team and management common terminology to ensure that everybody is on the same page when discussing prospects and opportunities. **This has little lasting impact if sales management doesn't adopt the new terminology and impress it in all of their conversations with the sales team and with senior management.** This happens too often.

One glaring example of this is how the organizations' CRM system is not updated to reflect either the new language for the adopted process or the new processes themselves that were taught in the sales training. This defeats the intent of the training and to a large extent helps to confuse the salespeople.

All of this time and energy invested in nomenclature, understanding of the buyer, and process is of little use if you, the salesperson, do not feel comfortable implementing these steps in front of the buyer.

Imagine someone playing sports having an inherent fear of being hurt. How good would a goalie or a defensive player be even if they understood all of the plays and all the processes in the game. Their "head would not be in the game". We know what happens to their playing time and to their career.

The biggest concern about sales training, quite frankly, is that it is always presented as a doing **to** the salesperson as opposed to a doing **for** the salesperson. How many sales people really view sales training as helping them achieve their goals?

Sales training is knowledge. It's hard to argue that increasing and improving your knowledge is bad for you. But knowledge not being accepted by the learner because of their Mindset reduces the effectiveness to almost zero.

"Who's the more foolish: the fool, or the fool who follows him?"

Obi Wan Kenobi

Salespeople are not comfortable disclosing their skills concerns to their sales manager

Let's start with a really interesting statistic. According to the Sales Benchmark Index, over 74% of sales managers admit they have poor communication skills. Communication is a two-way street. What this statistic tells us is that not only can sales managers not express themselves properly, but they don't understand the salesperson's perspective.

And since sales is all about money, here's another interesting statistic. According to a Holmes (a voice of the global PR industry) report, the cost of poor communication has hit an overwhelming $37 billion. Also, 400 surveyed corporations (with 100,000 plus employees in the U.S. and U.K.) estimated that communication barriers cost the average organization $62.4 million per year in lost productivity.

And according to Forbes, the cost of communication failure is most often exhibited in:

- Lack of Focus
- Failure to convey purpose
- Lack of innovation
- Drop in Morale
- Loss of Credibility

Little wonder why sales reps play "close to the vest".

Sales managers are people, plain and simple. And like normal people, too often, are scared of failure. Managers, especially sales managers, are pressured from above; their boss, and below; their salespeople.

THE CURRENT APPROACHES HAVE SHORTCOMINGS

Add the complexity that most sales managers are promoted from the ranks of salespeople and not due to their management or leadership skills. These managers were successful as sales reps.

And the better sales reps are successful without knowing specifically what makes them successful. So, the manager manages based upon trying to get their reps to emulate their behavior. Generally, this doesn't work as everybody is different. Many salespeople are drawn to sales because they (should) have to ability to determine their owns actions in achieving their assigned goals.

As the saying goes, "To a carpenter with a hammer, every problem looks like a nail."

As an example, sales managers track sales performance based on a time metric: deals closed in the month or quarter. This works if the sales cycle and sales process is consistent and defined through a repeatable process.

If a sales rep's quota is (as an example) $1million and the quota can be retired on a single deal with a single client, what is the benefit or justification of having the rep adhere to a monthly or quarterly quota achievement number?

Deal size does not necessarily correlate to a predetermined close frequency. A good rep would be penalized.

A rep selling the episodic single or few deals working for a manger focused on (or worse, being paid on) attainment to a time bound goal, would have conflict by design.

The probability of the rep being amenable to discussing strategy with their sales manager would be very low. And if the rep were successful, the chance that they would stay with the manager is very low.

> *"You've gotta dance like there's nobody watching, Love like you'll never be hurt, Sing like there's nobody listening, And live like it's heaven on earth."*
>
> **— William W. Purkey**

Thus, you should feel empowered because you now know where many of the potholes lurk. And I wouldn't tell you the bad if I wasn't going to tell you the good!

CHAPTER THREE

THE IMPACT TO YOU

On your earning power

Let's start by establishing some earnings guidelines. These are directional and not necessarily accurate for all jobs and markets.

Retail is typically the lowest paying employer with compensation often being close to minimum wage.

According to Payscale, the average Business Development Representative salary is $48,474 per year. The range for total pay is $33,000 to $80,000. BDR jobs have historically been considered entry level jobs, but that is changing.

Hubspot cites general sales jobs salaries average at $60,279 and commissions at $12,000.

While Glassdoor, lists the average base salary for a salesperson at $56,153 per year in the United States and $12,000 commission per year.

One of the highest compensated markets, due to cost of living and talent, is the New York City area where the average salary is $70,615 per year. This is in a range where the top end is $181,261. And these numbers do not include commissions.

In the technology and other fields, a compensation structure based on salary plus commission geared towards OTE (On Target Earnings) might be $120,000 base and an additional $120,000 at quota. Some companies will add incentives for over quota achievement, new name accounts, quarterly consistency, select product bonuses, and more.

Most compensation plans include some base salary and a commission or bonus based on either sales or percentage of quota. Usually, the commission or bonus is paid on a sliding scale based on the percentage of quota the rep has achieved. Once a sales rep has achieved their quota, many organizations will reward them with an escalated commission percentage.

Even moderately run organizations will seek to retain those reps achieving their quota and reward them for staying.

What would a 10% increase in earnings mean to you and your dreams? For one year? Over 10 years?

Companies are concerned with a reps' ability to generate revenue consistently and to fit into the corporate culture. Sales management is willing to make concessions to retain those salespeople. Sometimes it is more money, higher accelerators, stock options, etc.

The above numbers are enticing. I can tell you from personal experience that there are few feeling as good as receiving a 5-figure commission check!

But all this is dependent upon you being able to maintain that level of earning, or more.

In almost every selling position, with the probable exception of some retail, it can take weeks to months for a new rep to become productive and to generate commissions for themselves.

One 3- or 6-month stint without a source of income can significantly impact your earnings for the year and beyond. Especially if you do not have an emergency reserve fund.

You can also see that the ability to move 'up the food chain' in positions is based on how well you have achieved in your prior or current position. It is not uncommon for a salesperson to start in retail and quickly take on a BDR role and then a Territory Rep role and then an Account Executive role, etc.

There are quite a few sales professionals that earn more than their CEO.

All of this leads to one thought. This can be yours, or not, depending upon your performance. And your performance starts with your Mindset.

On your job

Sales, as a job, does not pay you for simply showing up. You are judged on your contribution to metrics such as quota, new revenue, margin, new accounts, etc. Not for how many hours you work.

For higher compensated positions, you have to work harder than many non-sales jobs.

Sales managers are constantly looking for those reps that can help them achieve their number and then do more, when required. And as you have seen from the stats on the percentage of reps that make quota, if you are a "Quota Buster", you'll be asked to do more - frequently.

When you struggle with sales and with consistent production, you will be 'under the microscope'. First your numbers will be watched. Then your activity metrics. Then the activities themselves. You will constantly be questioned, even grilled, to the point of becoming demoralized. (Refer back to the Shane Falco quote at the beginning of the **Introduction**.)

And as we have said earlier, since the majority of sales managers are lacking in management and leadership skills, their ability to help you as an individual is severely limited. The result being that they make decisions based on your inability to be successful because you cannot follow their path to success.

What about experience? The market considers experience in a specific role greater than 15 years to have no incremental value. Some organizations and mangers lower that number. This means that the path to success in sales requires you to learn and to grow your skills. You need to evolve to a more challenging role in order to continue expanding your earnings. If you haven't mastered lower-level skills and gained the appropriate knowledge, you will not progress. Your usefulness, and value in the market will stagnate.

Also, if you lose your job, you will spend 3 or 6 or more months both finding a new job and then having to relearn the product, market, internal process and internal political information to become successful.

Generally speaking, organizations hire individuals based upon what they have done that the organization wants them to repeat or based on what they can do as predicted by their past activities and successes. The best place to hone your skills and develop new ones is in a company where you are already comfortable. Impossible to do if you are not there!

On your family and self

I can attest to the immense satisfaction my wife and I derived from flying first class to an all-expense paid vacation in Hawaii as a result of exceeding my quota. Not just Hawaii but always at a Four Seasons resort. And when you were a repeat Achiever, they added an additional day to your trip.

There is very little to compare to a top-quality property: food, service, attitude and amenities. Yes, I worked hard during the year. But these trips helped make it worth the effort. The most rewarding aspect was knowing that my wife enjoyed these trips!

That's just one example of life when you're at your number. But the reverse is equally impactful.

When you're struggling, you're always wondering about your future. Always uncertain how to allocate your limited income. Waking up in the middle of the night angry because you want to provide for your family needs and dreams. Can you take a vacation, visit family, check off bucket list items? All the time wearing down your body's natural defenses against disease.

Some of the worst feelings come when you believe that your family feels let-down. When you feel they have lost faith in your ability to provide.

And then you start to envision your job and your career coming to an abrupt stop. Yes, you'll most likely survive a car crash, but it will take time and won't be fun.

We all have success metric clocks in our heads. Everyone has different reference points, and they are real to each of us. The more of these we miss or don't achieve, the more scared, frustrated, angry, and then less effective, we become.

As a Psychreg.org article on "How Job Loss Impacts Mental Health" states,

"When you lose your job, do you feel like you still have meaning in your life?

Unfortunately for many, losing their job may feel like the end of the world. Many individuals feel as though their success and worth are measured by being employed."

"The following are how job loss can impact your mental health:

1. You tend to feel more anxious

Anxiety is one of the more common results directly attributed to a job loss. When you no longer have a source of income, you become anxious about everything. How are you going to afford paying for your rent, meals, utilities? Are there medications that you have to pay for? How are you going to pay for the needs of your children and family?

2. You begin to develop self-doubt

Self-doubt is very common with individuals who have gone through a job loss. The longer it has been since their last employment, the more deep-seated their doubt becomes. Because you're unable to land a job immediately, you might begin to question your capabilities and skills.

3. You'll start to develop depression

When you're unemployed, there's a natural tendency to feel a sense of hopelessness. Others may feel disappointed in themselves. Some even disconnect from family and friends and may refuse to attend social gatherings because they're ashamed to be asked about where they're working or what they're currently doing – questions that often come up during conversations."

> *"Strength does not come from winning. Your struggles develop your strengths. When you go through hardships and decide not to surrender, that is strength."*
>
> **– Arnold Schwarzenegger**

In essence, sales is a mind game. The purpose of this chapter was to highlight the very dark, but very real, side of a poor Mindset. The more you know how to identify what you don't want, the easier it will be to focus on your success. We start that in the next chapter!

CHAPTER FOUR

INTRODUCING YOU

"The biggest wall you have to climb is the one you build in your mind: Never let your mind talk you out of your dreams, trick you into giving up. Never let your mind become the greatest obstacle to success. To get your mind on the right track, the rest will follow."

— Roy T. Bennett, <u>The Light in the Heart</u>

What is Mindset? Why is it important?

I think it is best to leave the definition of Mindset to experts. Here are a few descriptions from different sources

livepurposefullynow.com speaks of Mindset as

"Your Mindset is the single most vital factor influencing your life and it matters because your personal and professional success, happiness and wellbeing depend on your life perspective.

In other words, your Mindset underscores every aspect of life, from success to satisfaction.

Luckily for us all, we can fine-tune the inner conversations that lie at the core of our Mindset.

Make no mistake about it, your life experiences are directly related to every thought and feeling you have, and they have a powerful impact on your behavior and consequently your results. So, it's important to get this fundamental element right.

If you're serious about achieving your heart's desires in all or any area of your life, Mindset is the one thing you need to master."

According to an article in **verywellmind.com**, "Your Mindset is a set of beliefs that shape how you make sense of the world and yourself. It influences how you think, feel, and behave in any given situation."

American Heritage Dictionary of the English Language defines Mindset as:

"**1.** A fixed mental attitude or disposition that predetermines a person's responses to and interpretations of situations.

2. An inclination or a habit."

The following are 3 paragraphs from an article in **Psychology Today** that provide yet more color on the question of definition.

"A *Mindset* is a belief that orients the way we handle situations—the way we sort out what is going on and what we should do. Our Mindsets help us spot opportunities, but they can also trap us in self-defeating cycles.

This essay isn't about all the beliefs we might hold. It is about the beliefs that make a difference in our lives—the beliefs that distinguish people who are successful at what they do versus those who continually struggle.

Mindsets aren't just any beliefs. They are beliefs that orient our reactions and tendencies. They serve a number of cognitive functions. They let us frame situations: they direct our attention to the most important cues, so that we're not overwhelmed with information. They suggest sensible goals so that we know what we should be trying to achieve. They prime us with reasonable courses of action so that we don't have to puzzle out what to do. When our Mindsets become habitual, they define who we are, and who we can become."

There are many examples of the power or limitations of Mindset. Here's just one.

For very many years, the sports world believed that it was humanly impossible for a runner to cover a one mile distance in less than four minutes. Runners had been chasing the goal seriously since at least 1886.

There were scientific and psychological explanations as to the experts' logic and arguments. So, of course, no one did.

That is until May 6, 1954 when Roger Bannister ran the mile in 3:59.04. What was interesting was the makeup of the runner. According to an article in Harvard Business Review, "Bannister was an outlier and iconoclast — a full-time student who had little use for coaches and devised his own system for preparing to race. The British press "constantly ran stories criticizing his 'lone wolf' approach,"

Bryant notes, and urged him to adopt a more conventional regimen of training and coaching."

Roger was not impacted by the conventional Mindset of the day.

> *"The mind is the limit. As long as the mind can envision the fact that you can do something. You can do it, as long as you really believe 100 percent."*
>
> *– Arnold Schwarzenegger*

Who are you in your mind?

Our mind is an interesting and mysterious place.

Have you ever asked yourself, "Who am I?" Did you get an answer or just more questions? Do you see yourself as an introvert or an extrovert? A leader or a follower? Self-secure or insecure? A dog person or a cat person? Or neither?

Are you consistent in how you see yourself and how you react to situations?

I remember a friend of mind, on turning 40, said that the biggest difficulty he had was rationalizing what his mind said he could do vs what his body was allowing him to do.

What does this have to do with sales?

You have to understand yourself: your beliefs, your attitudes, your values, your work ethic, your style, and more if you want to be successful. The good news is that you don't have to know all of this before you can start to improve. But you have to start- now.

Consider this reality check from Jocko Willink, "There are people in the world who have skills and strength and talent that I will never have. Never. These notions that you can 'be whatever you want as long as you want it bad enough' are not true. They are fairy tales."

If you're not sure, and even if you think you are, it's worth taking a few of the personality profile test available for free or for a reasonable fee. These will give you a perspective of yourself. Do not rely on these as the only view. And remember that we as humans change over time. You may get some insight into unrealized possible strengths and some blind spots.

Let's talk about the other big hinderance for a large number of people. The notion of rejection. There's a lot of material written about this, but I would like to highlight one quick and effective strategy.

The issue starts with your fear of being rejected by your prospect or customer. Imaging then the person you would need to be, NOT to be impacted by your fear. How would the new you act? What would you say?

Once you have created your sales avatar, start to think that way and be that avatar. The avatar isn't your true self, it's a representation of a different aspect of you. Not if a prospect or customer rejects you, they are rejecting your avatar. And your ego stays intact.

It's important to always keep in mind that people don't see **you**. They see the version of you that you decide to show them. You have control over how you project **you**.

> *"Whether you think you can, or think you can't – either way you're right."*
>
> *– Henry Ford*

If you don't know you "Why", how can you make a decision?

Have you ever heard of James Lawrence? He's in the Guinness Book of World Records.

In 2015 he completed 50 Ironman Triathlon races, one in each of the 50 states of America, in a baffling 50 consecutive days.

A single Ironman distance event has a 3.86-km (2.4 miles) swim, 180.2-km (112 miles) bike ride and 42.16-km (26.2 miles – a Marathon distance) run.

James completed 50 of these grueling races without even a single day's break.

But you don't just wake up one morning and decide to accomplish a feat such as this. You need motivation. You need a reason – a Why. James' Why was to raise awareness about child obesity, a growing menace in the US.

But that wasn't enough. James adopted a new Why in 2021 and completed 100 races in 100 days. This time his Why was to raise awareness and funding against human trafficking.

Most of us have much more modest and realistic Whys. Maybe to set an example for their children, or to open a scholarship in someone's honor, or simply to be in the top 10% of their field or company.

The truth is that when we get tired or frustrated or discouraged, a clearly articulated Why will often times give us the energy to continue.

There is another reason understanding your Why is critical. Does achieving your Why correlate to the organization's goal and practices? Or will a conflict emerge?

As an example, part of achieving your Why might require that you are home with your children every night at a certain time. If you work for an organization that requires more flexibility and extended work hours, will this create an issue?

Truly understanding what is important to you will help you decide if a particular job is consistent with your plan. And will help you shape how you approach your work. Compromises will most likely have to be made. You need to know where and how.

> *"Working hard for something we do not care about is called stress, working hard for something we love is called passion."*
>
> **— *Simon Sinek***

I know I put a lot in this chapter. But are you starting to get the sense that this is really all up to you? And that you CAN do it?

CHAPTER FIVE

Understanding Your Market

One demonstration of developing trust is understanding business issues your prospect experiences. This is not meant to imply that you become an expert in their industry. Rather, that spending some time educating yourself on a few of these aspects will allow you to have more effective conversations with them and will facilitate trust in a shorter timeframe.

Having an understanding of these concepts will help you appreciate the concerns of your prospect. You can then discuss your offerings in the context of their challenges in the marketplace.

Characteristics of Your Target Market

We'll introduce four of these below, but it is your responsibility to invest the time to conduct your own research.

1 - Products have life cycles.

We'll use the term "Products" to mean an organization's offerings whether they be hard goods, software, services, etc. Those life cycles are related to when and how the product was introduced into the market and when and how 'consumers' adopted it. The Market Acceptance Curve or Product Life Cycle Curve speaks to differences in marketing, selling, pricing and the Mindset of the buyers in each of the stages. Some writers will refer to this as the Technology Adoption Curve.

Your buyer's organization will have different needs, possibly for the same offering, based on where they are in this cycle.

You should also understand this for the product(s) you are selling. It will aid in understanding your organization's needs and objectives.

2 - Every industry is impacted by multiple forces. Competition, regulation, market maturity, globalism, talent availability, and more. These forces shape the goals and objectives of the decision makers, and their reports, that you are trying to influence. Your ability to interrupt their day is in part dependent on your understanding their priorities (challenges) and shaping your selling message to them.

3 – Compensation plays an outsized role in anyone's decision making. Would you continue working for your organization if your compensation structure was modified? Maybe not.

If you understand how your prospects are compensated, you'll understand where they are expected to, and where they will, place their energy. That will inform you on what types of solutions will best assist them. And how you should frame the value proposition.

4 – Their Lifecycle and Lifestyle. People in general are risk adverse. It doesn't mean we don't take them but will assess their severity and

likelihood of a negative outcome. Humans will make decision based first upon their needs and then upon the needs of the organization.

Lifecycle refers to where in their career they are now and what decisions they will make vs those they will avoid. An executive a few years from retirement may not want to embark on a project that will add work to his/her daily schedule. There is no benefit, potentially, to them. Whereas another individual may want to accomplish certain goals, for personal or professional reason, and is willing to take a chance on your solution.

Lifestyle speaks to someone's approach to life. There are different personality types and numerous ways to classify them. The value of this knowledge is being able to tailor your proposition not just based on the organization's parameters, but also on the individual's.

> *"You can make more friends in two months by becoming interested in other people than you in two years by trying to get other people interested in you."*
>
> ***Dale Carnegie***

What are you selling vs delivering

BMW doesn't 'sell' cars. They sell "The Ultimate Driving Machine". They deliver you a car.

Mercedes Benz says, "The three-pointed star doesn't just identify a Mercedes-Benz. It represents over a century of tradition, a commitment to quality, and a promise to always shine brighter than ever before." They deliver a car.

Or Audi's, "Truth in Engineering".

They sell an image, an experience, a promise, exclusivity, elitism, convenience, status, and more.

Look at the watch manufacturer Patek Philippe positioning, ""You never actually own a Patek Philippe. You merely look after it for the next generation."

MasterCard works to convince you that, "There Are Some Things Money Can't Buy. For Everything Else, There's Mastercard."

All too often when salespeople are asked what they sell, they regress into a product description complete with features and marketing's perceived benefits. Little wonder why buyers have no interest in speaking with sales reps and prefer to conduct their research online.

Buyers may look for functionality and usefulness but will make their decision based upon emotional inputs. The examples above were developed after extensive research and market testing to determine resonance with the organizations' target audience.

The easiest way to internalize this message is that people buy to solve a problem that causes them emotional concern or stress. The problem is due to a technical lack or shortcoming in the organization. They buy based on their needs and rationalize based on the organization's needs.

Increasing revenue or decreasing expenses may be the organization's stated needs, but there are reasons behind why they feel it necessary to accomplish these things.

I was speaking with a firm recently that had the stated objective of increasing their pricing. They claimed it was to increase revenue. We could have focused on that.

But when asked why increasing revenue was important, they admitted that at the current revenue (and importantly, margin) levels, they were not able to adequately pay the top executives. Their bigger and primary concern was losing their key talent. Not simply revenue.

This enabled us to have a more in depth and impactful discussion and focus on real needs.

Again, no silver bullets here. Just a way for you to reshape your Mindset that helps the buyer prefer doing business with you over your competitors.

"Try not to become a person of success, but try to become a person of value."

– *Albert Einstein*

What is the Mindset and Projection needed to be successful

We'll summarize some earlier points and add more to address this

First – Decide if you really want to be a sales professional. Not just try it out or do it because you don't know what you want to do for your life. And if you do, then commit to work at your craft. Your commitment and dedication will project itself to your prospects and customers. It will give you clarity and that will project outward in a positive way.

Second - As written in a **cueinsights.com** article, "A research study, published in *Psychological Science*, found that it takes less than a second for somebody to judge another person during their first encounter. Trustworthiness, status and attractiveness are immediately assessed during a first impression."

This is reinforced by Malcolm Gladwell in his book "Blink: The Power of Thinking Without Thinking" where he states, "Buyers make most decisions by relying on their two-second first impressions based on stored memories, images and feelings,"

The guidance here is that you have to be 100% on your "A game" when you first encounter a prospect or buyer. And don't be misled to believe that it only applies to in person meetings. First impressions are easily made via telephone calls or Social Media presence.

Third (and highly correlated to the Second) – It is often said that customers buy from people they like. While we don't usually buy from people we dislike, there is one more dimension to this old saying. And that is that Customers buy from people they trust.

The interesting distinction is that the saying refers to "customers" but the reality is that this holds true with prospects. The dynamic is different in that you have less time, typically, to build that trust. But that's a topic for another time as it is quite complex.

For now, act in a trustworthy manner. Little things like not lying help your cause. If you don't know, for example, just say so.

Fourth – As has been discussed in a prior section, don't "show up and throw-up". Help the prospect solve their problem.

Remember the words of Jeffrey Gitomer, "People don't like to be sold, but they love to buy." Let them.

Fifth – This is so true regardless of who said it originally, "People will forget what you said. People will forget what you did. But people will never forget how you made them feel."

There is so much more and such nuance to all of these points. But this is a good place to start. If you notice, there are no Tricks or Hacks here. Most of this is common sense and easily applied. It just takes time and practice.

> *"The three great essentials to achieve anything worthwhile are, first, hard work; second, stick-to-itiveness; third, common sense."*
>
> — ***Thomas A. Edison***

Please note that none of the above are 'silver bullets'. They are simply tactics to help you improve your position with the prospect by improving your perspective of the value you bring. In short, this will strengthen your Mindset.

CHAPTER SIX

What YOU Bring to the Table

You can be, and depending upon the type of sales in which you engage, will be a very influential factor in the decision process of your buyer. That's a good thing!

People Buy YOU

You have the potential to be a tremendous resource to your prospects / customers. Because you and your organization speak with and solve problems for your prospect's competitors, you have a unique view of their market.

Also, because of the same above reasons, you have the ability to share best practices with your buyers.

You see use cases for your offerings, every day. While your prospect / customer only sees their own use case.

The only reason a prospect would be speaking with you is because they have a problem they would like to solve. They may not be willing to divulge their concerns immediately. You might have to gain that right. None the less, they do have an issue.

It is possible that the prospect may only need to quantify the extent of their concern, so they can prioritize the solution. That in and of itself is of value.

Any problem or issue an organization may be facing where they need to seek outside advice is, to them, a weakness.

We discussed in the prior chapter the notion that people make decisions about other people in very short time frames. The quicker you can relate to the prospect and have them initially feel that they can trust you, the sooner they will honestly discuss their concerns.

Have you ever had a brief conversation or meeting with someone, and you got the immediate feeling that "they got you"? Remember how good that felt?

Committing to purchasing a product or service may, depending upon the price and complexity, can be confusing and intimidating. Consider that purchasing your offering may have cost and resource allocation ramifications within the prospect's organization that they do not fully comprehend.

Realize that one benefit you may bring to the table is the understanding of the total impact of implementing your solution. You are in a position to gain the trust and reduce the stress by providing the customer with a roadmap to success. You have done this before. The customer may not have.

Consider the decision-making process. There are many variations on this, so spend some time to understand the process and where you can add value for your prospect.

Every decision has these components in some form or another.

Here are 2 versions:

Version one

- Need recognition
- Information Gathering
- Solution Evaluation and Evaluation Criteria creation
- Solution Choice and Purchase
- Buyers Remorse or "Second Guessing"
- Implementation and Adoption into Workflow
- Purchase Decision Justification

Version two

- Recognizing the challenge / problem
- Developing the justification
- Gaining Organizational Agreement
- Find Qualified Providers
- Information Gathering and Provider Assessment
- Purchase Terme and Conditions Negotiation
- Performance Assessment of Providers

The more complex the purchase, the more complex the buying process. By understanding the steps, you can ensure the prospect is aware and makes a smooth decision.

> *"Successful people are always looking for opportunities to help others. Unsuccessful people are always asking, What's in it for me?"*
>
> *– Brian Tracy*

Buyers Have Choices

One of the most frustrating aspect of sales management is when a deal is lost, the salesperson immediately writes in the Lost Report, "Our price was too high".

Besides being arguably a feeble attempt on the part of the salesperson to truly understand and admit why the opportunity didn't mature, it's a sign of overall weak sales culture and poor management. Let's look at four factors, on the prospect's side, too often overlooked or forgotten.

Virtually every purchase has an additional impact from **internal costs**. The "cost" of the product or service from the salesperson's perspective is perceived to be fully represented by the bottom-line number on the quotation. This is far from the truth.

There are internal costs associated with staffing, reallocation of resources, additional products and/or services required to implement your solution, lost opportunity costs, cost of capital, and more. All of these become components of the calculation to determine the actual cost of the project.

You as the salesperson may not see these but it is a significant mistake not to be aware, and cautious, of their existence.

No decision is a choice. As we mentioned earlier, there are unknowns in any decision. Some are known unknowns, and some are unknown unknowns. It is not uncommon for decision makers and organizations to be concerned enough about what they know they **don't know** to decide to not move forward. It doesn't mean your offering was deficient, only your selling process.

The lure of a better future. Capital expenditures, by definition, have an extended life expectancy. Three, five, ten or more years is not uncommon. Translated, a decision today could still haunt the buyer and the organization in 15 years. That's a sobering thought.

It's not an uncommon tactic for a selling organization to announce or even pre-announce the "next big thing". The intent is to stop the prospect from making a buy decision, today, that takes them off the market for an extended period of time.

One of the benefits to the selling organization is that if they know that their offering is of lesser value to the prospect, by pre-announcing they have the opportunity to collect feedback from the prospect and tweak their offering.

Buyers have **multiple projects they are trying to fund** and accomplish. And as the organization size increases and depending on where they are in their product lifecycle, there can be a mind-numbing number of projects competing.

The C Suite has to consider the organization's total needs as well as juggle the personalities and desires of their senior staff. At the end of the day, these people make the organization work.

Your prospect, individually, could have multiple priorities for a limited amount of budget under their control. And they are always in competition with their peers for the total limited resources of the organization. Its just the way business is run – your competition could be a project with a higher ROI.

Your job is to uncover these factors and help guide your prospect towards success with your offering.

"Stop selling. Start helping."

– Zig Ziglar

Your product & company's view of the market

All products and services are created based on a perceived need in the market. Someone, usually the founder, believed that "there's got to be a better way" and went about researching, creating, testing, failing, and starting again on a solution. During the process, he/she/they discovered many approaches that didn't work and refined aspects they at first believed to be adequate.

As the famous Thomas Edison quote on developing the electric light bulb reads, "I have not failed. I've just found 10,000 ways that won't work."

What makes this so powerful is the realization that your organization (or you if you are the entrepreneur) has spent more time and focused energy on not just solving the problem but on understanding the root cause and the ramifications of its impact. Much more so than the prospect organization as their concern, rightly so, is to mitigate the impact to their goals. They are not in the business of solving the problem.

Thus, potentially what your organization brings to the table is a vastly deeper expertise than the prospect could ever hope to realize. Unfortunately, all too often salespeople and their management forget the value of this knowledge. It is a competitive advantage and a differentiating perspective!

This advantage, if nurtured and harvested properly, should only continue to grow.

As your organization continues to speak with prospects, get feedback from customers, compare notes with other organizations in their ecosystem, attend conferences and meetings, and compile salespeople's notes, more and more insights are gleaned. Again, much more than the prospect could or would ever compile on their own.

"People will buy anything that is one to a customer"

*– **Sinclair Lewis***

So, are you feeling your superpowers emerge?

CHAPTER SEVEN

Game Changing Perspectives

Everything we have been discussing so far is about your Mindset. It's the most powerful weapon under YOUR control.

There are many strategies and tactics available to you. What follows are three you may find relatively straightforward to understand and to deploy. Your immediate reaction may be to say that the implementation of these requires more departments and individuals in your organization to embrace them. That's not necessarily true. Yes, depending upon your organization and functional structure, multiple groups could be involved.

The Red Velvet Rope Policy

Red velvet ropes – you see them on the awards shows on TV. At nightclubs, political events, grand openings. Anywhere the intent is to let people know they either belong there, or they don't. It signals who gets admission and who stays outside.

Michael Port in his excellent book, "Book Yourself Solid", highlights this notion very clearly. Below is an excerpt from a book summary. The highlights are mine.

"To begin the process of getting more clients, first **weed out your current ones that are draining you**. It's scary to let go of clients when you need money, but having a red velvet rope policy like the bouncer at an exclusive club helps you **focus on those who have potential for growth**. When you hang out with great people and get rid of energy drains, the contagious sense of high energy will spill over into your work.

Create a velvet rope policy by **identifying the ideal traits of your clients**. Focus on quality and avoid taking on anyone who isn't a good fit. Categorize your current clients into three groups: ideal, duds and everyone else. **Review which clients you love working with and why**. The clients in the ideal category will help you define your specific target market for attracting new business."

There is a wealth of information in the book. This should give you insight into the strategy.

As you can see, YOU can implement this approach with little or no assistance from anyone else in your organization.

> *"Not all readers are leaders, but all leaders are readers."—*
> **Harry S. Truman**

The Raving Fans notion

Here is another extremely compelling approach to acquire and retain customers. The following is from a **shortform.com** summary of the 1993 book, "Raving Fans: A Revolutionary Approach To Customer Service"

"In *Raving Fans*, management experts Ken Blanchard and Sheldon Bowles argue that successful organizations have one common central focus: **providing an excellent customer service experience**. And that any type of organization or business that serves people can benefit from these principles to create "Raving Fans."

Happy Customers Are Core to Your Success

According to the authors, whatever work you do, the people you serve are central to your success. Happy customers can share positive reviews with thousands of people. Likewise, disgruntled customers can write terrible reviews, can damage your reputation, and won't hesitate to abandon you for your competitors. With one click, your customers have the power to make or break you.

Blanchard and Bowles argue that there's a clear distinction between satisfying your customers and exceeding the expectations of your customers. If you merely seek to satisfy your customers, they'll only stay with you as long as you're not worse than the competition.

The authors argue that, in contrast, happy customers are likely to:

- Become loyal customers and offer a reliable source of revenue
- Promote your business by becoming brand advocates and help grow your customer base

- Offer feedback and a deeper understanding of their motivations, which will help you to create better products and services
- Test or become early adopters of your latest products and services"

I will tell you that of the three points mentioned in this Chapter, this is the one I have used most effectively to generate millions of dollars in sales!

> *"Competition whose motive is merely to compete, to drive some other fellow out, never carries very far. The competitor to be feared is one who never bothers about you at all, but goes on making his own business better all the time."*
>
> *-- Henry Ford*

The Discipline of Market Leaders

Focus creates market differentiation and competitive advantage. This strategy is very powerful however does require more assistance from other parts of the organization. You will still benefit from understanding and implementing the principles.

Michael Treacy and Fred Wiersema published "The Discipline of Market Leaders" in 1995. The specifics of their strategy are possibly even more relevant today and the concept of a differentiating approach will always be current.

They contend that market leaders have accepted the fact that they cannot be best in everything. Instead, they propose, that the organization needs to decide which of these dimensions of value they will claim as their differentiator. The three are price, innovation, and service. These need to be further defined.

Being the low-price leader is a competitive advantage principally in a low differentiated market.

Many organizations strive to leverage leading edge solutions. They are the early adopters.

And other firms see service as their path to customer acquisition, retention, and growth.

The authors continue to explain that market leaders must excel in one of the three dimensions of value while maintaining threshold standards on the other two values. There is more to their book, and it is worth the read.

From your perspective as a salesperson, you need to decide with of these dimensions you can reasonably claim as your organization's lead, and which gives you differentiation against your competitors. Sometimes simply highlighting the importance of a dimension, when the competition does not make that distinction, is enough to influence the buy decision in your direction.

> *"If you're not making mistakes, you're not taking risks, and that means you're not going anywhere. The key is to make mistakes faster than the competition, so you have more changes to learn and win."*
>
> *-- **John W. Holt, Jr.***

When you realize that your job as a salesperson is to be the primary interface between your organization and the prospect and customer, it means you are responsible for a significant part of the messaging to them. Instead of seeing these as difficult to implement, view them as challanges to yourself. Ask, "What would I have to do to make these a reality?"

CHAPTER EIGHT

Caring Counts

People making decisions are simply more vulnerable. And they know it. Consider all the variables they need to contend with including questions such as:

- Does the seller have my best interests at heart
- Is the seller lying to me
- Can this company really give me what I need
- What don't I know about their business practices
- Will the installation / implementation be as smooth as the salesman is telling me
- What wasn't disclosed in the costs
- Will this organization be around in three years
- Does the salesperson really care about me or just my deal.

The buyer knows they might not get true answers to most of these questions. Especially if this is the first time they are dealing with the seller and their organization. But, they have to make a decision because they need the product or service.

And people being what they are, will oftentimes make the buying process - for the seller - more difficult because of the buyer's unspoken fears and concerns. This makes your job harder.

What the buyer is really trying to figure out is if can they trust you and if you care about them. Let's look at some ways you can convey this to the buyer.

Show caring

Deliver Clarity

Arrange important facts in a clear and concise manner. Present them in a way that is clear to the buyer, not to you. Show details. Separate one-time from recurring costs. Illustrate the impact of choosing and not choosing the options of your solution.

Document

Put virtually everything you and the buyer discuss in writing. Then review with the buyer to ensure their understanding and agreement. Pay particular attention to next steps, timing, and responsibility.

Deliver good news

Give your customers and prospects **reasons to celebrate** such as early delivery, earlier delivery times, higher quality service, pricing considerations and more. Even the simple act of communicating information to them in a timely and positive manner, gets you credit. Did their order get approved? Tell them.

Deliver bad news fast

But when things go off the rails, remember that your customer has made plans **based upon your representations**.

When shipments get delayed, or prices get raised, mistakes are made in the quoting, or any number of actions that would cause your prospects' plans to be disrupted, **they want to know**.

Be complementary

The buyer is still a human with emotions. Treat them as such.

Ask for clarification / understand impact

Do not assume you know what is on the mind of the buyer. Take a moment to discuss with the intent of ensuring you and the buyer are in agreement concerning expectations, timelines, and roles. The nature of the English language allows for different meaning in our words. Too often our definition is not the same as the buyer's.

Understand constraints

What is your buyer's world like? To whom are they responsible? Most buyers have guidelines and rules under which they must operate and make decisions. Many have budget thresholds above which they need to gain additional approval. Many work within committee structures when contemplating acquisitions and spending funds.

These may impact your buyer's ability to make a decision and impact the timing of that decision. Telling them about yet more features will not help them address their internal issues. Work to understand them and find ways to address them. Or at a minimum, try.

Understand perspective

A fascinating and baffling reality of police work is that if they take eyewitness accounts of an incident, they will have as many variations of the "truth" as they have eyewitnesses.

Everybody has a viewpoint, and all believe theirs is accurate. It's no different for your buyer. They see things a certain way, regardless of your amazing features!

They are happy to explain and discus their viewpoint with you, if they feel it is in their best interests. Ask.

Help prospect sell up and across

As we discussed above in "Understand constraints", your buyer has other approvals they need in order to move the deal forward. You may have convinced the buyer, and now their work begins.

Discus with them what data they need and how they would present that data. Then spend time with your buyer to ensure they are comfortable with the data and its meanings. And that they can convey it compellingly.

Empathize

If you're getting the sense that the buyer has to spend a considerable amount of time, energy, resources, and maybe political capital to close on your deal, you're correct!

Sometimes we all could benefit from someone simply recognizing that it is a lot of work.

> *"Nobody cares how much you know, until they know how much you care."*
>
> — ***Theodore Roosevelt***

In-house Caring Counts as well

The first point above illustrates the benefit of being empathetic to the needs, styles, constraints and desires of others. In this case, we focused on the buyer.

But how much more, or more easily, could you accomplish your goals if you treated your co-workers with the same attention to their needs, etc.?

Almost none of us could complete our tasks successfully, and not in a best-of-class manner, without the assistance of a support team. It is simple, if you help your team on a daily basis, they will come to your assistance when you need it. Who wouldn't help a friend?

In my experience, two of the most underappreciated roles in an organization are Accounting and Legal. And yet you would be hard pressed to create and nurture a successful, long-term relationship with a significant client without their assistance. A kind word, a lunch, some recognition, doesn't take much from your day, but pays dividends.

Another little recognized dynamic is that when your prospect / customer needs to interact with your team members, the prospect / customer can sense the extent of your team's relationship and opinion of you. When they sense a feeling of camaraderie and mutual respect, they will feel more comfortable dealing with you and your organization. Weird how that works!

> *"Caring about people, about things, about life – is an act of maturity."*
>
> — *Tracy McMillan*

Long term relations

Depending upon how you, as the point person for your organization, structure a long term relationship with a client, you may have the opportunity to engage the client in more strategic and future oriented discussions. People tend to trust others more as the bank of positive experiences increases. The more a client is comfortable that you are honest and caring the more they will include you in conversation and decision where you will have the competitive advantage and edge.

This is not a position to take lightly. But you must be willing to do the work, and that can be difficult and stressful.

I was selling a top tier healthcare payer account. In an update meeting, my client contact informed me that their organization was looking to reduce the number of technology vendors with whom they were contracting. The feeling of management was that it was taking too much time and energy to manage a large number of vendors, and if they reduced the vendor number, the remaining vendors would have a larger incentive to price properly and deliver better results.

My organization was being asked to become one of these selected vendors due to the "care and feeding" my team had consistently delivered to the client. Not only did the revenue from the account increase, but the margins did as well. Also, the time to close new opportunities was reduced.

Sales is a relationship and trust game. NOT a report exercise. It is no different than your day-to-day life and interactions. All it takes is one wrong action to destroy that trust.

The core concept here is that we as salespeople, have to earn the trust of the buyer in both the initial sale and for subsequent transactions.

> *"The trees which are pruned, watered and nurtured by caring hands bear the greatest fruits; it is the same with people."*
>
> *— Bryant McGill*

CHAPTER NINE

You'll Walk Like a Superhero

Up to now we've talked about all the work you need to do and the reasons behind the logic. Now let's really talk about the payoff for you. How your life will be different!

How much more effective would you be if you had less stress?

Let's talk about stress and its effect on you.

According to an article in **lifeadvancer.com** titled "The Effects of Stress on Your Health and Well-Being: What You Need to Know",

"Stress has been linked to increased **rates of heart disease, digestive issues, asthma, and various types of addiction.**

"There are many symptoms associated with heightened levels of stress, including difficulty sleeping, trouble focusing on tasks, body tension, fatigue, and a variety of illnesses with no apparent physical cause. As the effects of stress become more severe, people can also become angry more easily and may notice more frequent headaches.

"These symptoms may be as benign as being slightly more tired at night or less interested in things one typically enjoys such as spending time with friends or watching television."

Other effects of stress listed in various sources include

- Headaches
- High blood pressure
- Upset stomach
- Tension
- Chest pains
- Anxiety
- Irritability
- Sadness
- Feeling overwhelmed

Long term stress has a direct link to:

- Heart disease
- Other cardiovascular conditions
- Difficulty in managing obesity and diabetes

And there's more!

The intent here is not to provide medical advice on reducing stress and improving your health. The objective is to help you understand the potential impact stress can have on you and to discuss what you would gain by eliminating even some stress.

Recent research has determined that we do not have the ability to focus on two tasks simultaneously. Efficiency and effectiveness are both sacrificed.

Think for a moment how that relates to worry and work. Or preoccupation and results. The issue at hand is that if your attitude / Mindset is not confident about your role as a professional salesperson, you will be stressed to some degree. The worse your position relative to quota, earnings, advancement, security, etc., the more anxiety you will experience. When you are in such a state, you CAN NOT focus 100% of your attention and energy on being successful in sales.

And this is stress related to one single aspect of your life. You will still have internal pressure from everyday factors such as your children, family, personal obligations, relatives, etc.

I ask you again, how would your professional life be different without this stress?

> *"In times of stress, the best thing we can do for each other is to listen with our ears and our hearts and to be assured that our questions are just as important as our answers."*
>
> *— Fred Rogers*

More resources to care for yourself and your family

Our families are our most intense reason for us to get up every morning and face the world. They are why we work the hours, days, weeks, and years. Their happiness, safety and security are paramount to most of us sales professionals.

Two of the three largest expense items we encounter in life are housing and education. Let's look at some statistics on these so you can develop a sense of what a relatively small increase in your earning could mean to your lifestyle and to your self-confidence.

In the words of Leonard Boswell, "The American Dream is one of success, home ownership, college education for one's children, and have a secure job to provide these and other goals."

Housing

The American dream is to own a single-family house. A home in which to watch the children grow, hold Holiday gatherings, cook burgers in the backyard, and make new friends in the neighborhood.

According to a **msn.com** article, "as of August 2021, a typical single-family home in the United States costs $303,288. Of course, home values are not uniform across the country, and in some states, the typical home costs far more than the national average -- while in others, homes cost far less."

The chart in the article showed that Hawaii had the highest cost at $764,146 while West Virginia had the lowest at $118,581. A very interesting aspect of the data in the chart is the comparison of the column "Value of a typical single-family home" compared to the column "Median household income". When comparing these 2 data points, they show that it takes from 9.2 times the income to afford a house in a particular state (Hawaii) to 2.43 times in another state (West Virginia). The average is 4.78. One way to interpret this data is that, on average, for every $10,000 increase in your income, you could afford $40,780 more in house value.

Home theater anyone?

College Education

A Forbes article in **forbes.com/finance** states, "College Costs Could Total As Much As $334,000 In Four Years"

"The most expensive colleges today are elite private colleges at $68,000 per year. While the rate of increase in college costs has slowed, the price is still going up. If your child is going to college four years from now (2018), the projected cost of an elite college from 2018 -- 2021 could soar as high as $334,000 for a four-year degree. The national average cost of attending a four-year public college is over $28,000 per year, and the average cost of attending a four-year private college is now over $59,000."

Now add to those numbers information as reported by **whattobecome.com** reporting on college scholarships:

"Fascinating Scholarship Facts and Stats (Editor's Pick)

- The average scholarship is worth $7,400.
- Only 0.2% of students got $25,000 or more in scholarships per year.
- The NCAA awards more than $2.9 billion in athletics scholarships annually.
- Only 1.3% of athletes receive a full or partial athletic scholarship."

That leaves a considerable number of deals for you to close to ensure your child(ren) receive the education you want them to have. Of course, this assumes that college is the correct choice for your child. But trade schools are not inexpensive, either.

<u>We'll add one more real-life expense just for illustration.</u>

A **valuepenguin.com** article covering the Average Cost of Weddings states, "Depending on where you get married, the cost of your wedding can vary significantly. Across the country, the average cost of a wedding was $20,300, but the cost can vary by as much as $18,063 depending on the state in which the ceremony and reception take place."

For some sales professionals, the cost of a wedding is equal to their commission on one good sized deal!

> *"I never truly understood the meaning of warmth until I purchased my own home. As I sit in my own living room, surrounded by walls painted my favorite color, looking out at the mighty oak tree sitting on the lot I so carefully chose and listening to the tranquil sounds of jazz music on my stereo, my soul is filled with deep contentment, a warmth that I could not before have fathomed."*
>
> *– Anonymous*

Plan more into the future

This point is relatively simple. If you were able to gain confidence in yourself you will be able to leverage the sales training, readings, product knowledge, guidance from others, and any other methodology to increase your effectiveness and efficiency. You will develop a consistency in achieving your goals and your numbers.

This consistency, tempered with some common sense in how you live, will allow you to bank your earnings and grow a nest egg for either a rainy day or for whatever you would like to achieve next in your life.

You also get recognized for your consistency by the market you serve and by your employers. This in of itself will greatly ensure that you are able to continue increasing your earnings over time. It has been said that the top 20% in any field never have to look for work.

If you are able to focus more, and more successfully, on achieving your goals you will be able to see your future more clearly and, in actuality, be able to determine it.

At the end of the day isn't this what you are aiming to accomplish?

> *"With patience and persistence, even the smallest act of discipleship or the tiniest ember of belief can become a blazing bonfire of a consecrated life. In fact, that's how most bonfires begin - as a simple spark."*
>
> ***Dieter F. Uchtdorf***

So, is your future looking brighter?

CHAPTER TEN

Expense Paid Vacations in Hawaii Aren't Too Shabby

A salesperson has a cost to an organization. Depending upon when the salesperson reaches a cost break even for their employer, the remainder of the revenue the salesperson generates will contribute profit to the organization in increasing amounts and percentages. A salesperson is worth considerably more to an employer the higher the revenue and margin they contribute.

Given the declining percentage of sales reps that achieve their quota, the more valuable those that do achieve quota are to the organization. Thus, organizations incentivize salespeople not simply to achieve their quota, but to surpass it.

Companies reward their high achievers in different ways

Compensation

There is no consistency in compensation structures for salespeople. They are designed to help the organization achieve their objectives through sales, and as such will differ by design. Any organization that hires an employee needs to get a return on that employee's effort. This is no different in sales.

The one difference with salespeople is that the more they sell the more revenue, and typically margin, the organization can realize. As is true with any other employee, there is a certain fixed cost associated with their employment. However most other employees do not have the ability to generate income and margin.

In most organizations, the more the salesperson sells the higher the organization's percentage of margin increases. It is then in the best interest of the organization to motivate the salesperson to sell more than their quota.

Many organizations will structure their compensation package to incentivize the salesperson to sell over and above quota. The Commission percentage will increase as the salesperson's bookings exceed their target. It is not uncommon for a salesperson to double their projected commission earnings by exceeding their target.

Trips

A common incentive for salespeople is an expense paid vacation, for themselves and sometimes their family, if the salesperson achieves a certain percentage of quota. These are typically referred to as Quota Achievers Club or Presidents Club. The qualifying salespeople are treated to an all-expense paid few days at a desirable destination or vacation spot. Hawaii, Bermuda, the Bahamas, Mexico are all popular choices.

Spiffs

Another frequently used motivation technique is to provide rewards tied to some specific activity. Usually, the activity is revenue or specific product oriented. The prize might be a gift certificate to a high-end restaurant for the salesperson who sells the most in a given day. Or a company-paid lease on a Mercedes-Benz or Porsche for two years for a top performing salesperson.

If an organization is attempting to introduce a new product to the market, they may create a special incentive for the salesperson who generates the most sales on that product. These types of incentive programs are utilized to motivate the team as well as increase revenue. And often times can be fun for the salespeople.

Besides, flying first class with your spouse to an all-expense paid week in Hawaii in February it's not the worst thing that could happen to you!

> *"If you believe in yourself and have dedication and pride - and never quit, you'll be a winner. The price of victory is high but so are the rewards."*
>
> **- Bear Bryant**

You will have exposure to executives

Look at it from management's perspective. Top selling sales reps can be a valuable source of information to the organization. They want to get to know who you are and understand what you do and why you're successful. Not only are you contributing to the organization but realistically you're helping fund management's bonuses. They want to protect that. So, they want to talk to you.

They want to understand your accounts: why they buy, what value they see in your organization's products and services, while they chose you versus your competitor, what would they need to spend more money with you, and lots more. If you're selling at a high level in an account, you have access to the C-Suite and your management wants to leverage that.

An important part of any organization that's developing products for the market is to have a client base of knowledgeable users that are willing to be beta customers. These customers are invaluable to your organization because they help guide and shape the development of new products as well as the pricing of those products. If you're at the top of the game, you have access to those potential beta customers. Product development and product marketing want to be your best friend.

Speak to one customer and you have a personal preference, but speak to a number and you have insight into a market direction.

More enlightened executives will court their top salespeople for their insight. If that's you, don't be surprised if you get invitations to special meetings, lunches, dinners, strategy sessions, golf games and fun offsites. These executives understand not only the value of your perspective on how to get clients to buy but also on your ability to introduced them to networks of decision makers and influencers.

The better executives also understand that it is you that holds the relationship between the customer and your organization in good stead. They understand that loss of a good account executive has a high probability of meaning the loss of the customer. Considering that it takes more time, energy, and money to gain a new customer then to retain one, it's actually a better business decision to keep you happy.

The flip side to this, and what makes this so interesting and powerful, is that if you position yourself properly with the executives, you get to ask for things.

Go accept that invitation for a ride on the corporate jet!

> *"You need fans in high places, I always tell people. I don't care how talented you are."*
>
> *- Jaleel White*

The top 20% never have to look for a job

The 80/20 rule does apply. 80% of the revenue is generated by 20% of the salespeople. Organizations and sales management understand this. Good sales managers know of the salespeople from other organizations – their competition. A top 20% salesperson is not only hard to find but even harder to entice to make a move and organizations will make room on their team for these high achievers.

Look at it from the sales manager's perspective. If they are able to take a top 20% salesperson from a competitor, they lessen their competitive threat. A very desirable bonus!

As was mentioned above, high achieving salespeople generate not just additional revenue but increased profit for their organization.

Organizations and sales managers are constantly on the lookout for high achievers they can add to their team.

Once you become a top 20 percenter your name will be on somebody else's list and very likely you will be approached again and again from the organization or from headhunters.

Markets change, products change, management changes, competitors change. You never know when being in the top 20% is going to come in handy to help speed your transition to a new and potentially better position.

Its nice to be in demand!

> *"Don't overlook the money part of it. I've been poor and I've been rich. Rich is better!"*
>
> **- Mrs. George S. Kaufman**

Let me say it again, it's nice to be in demand!

CONCLUSION

Hey there! I'm glad to see you made it this far. I hope that means you're finding value in this and that you really are looking to better your life.

Why Change?

It's always a great question. Why should I go through a change? It's painful. It takes time. I'm out of my comfort zone. YIKES!

Well, the answer is actually kind of simple. If we want something, we have to actually work to get it. We learned this growing up from our parents, from our schoolteachers, from our friends, from books and movies, and maybe even from our pastor. If we don't change, we can't have a change in our life and our tomorrows.

Since you have stayed interested this far in the book, I have to believe that there are certain things you want in life. Maybe it's more income, a degree of certainty, a better future not just for yourself but for your family, or maybe it's just to be a better salesperson.

But the task, at this point, is not to make all the changes, now. It is not to try to become a completely different person in a very short period of time. Because that simply isn't going to happen. What we have been talking about throughout this book encompasses our Mindset and behavior changes. Who we are is based upon everything that's happened in our life, up to now. You can't remake yourself overnight.

The task now is to start the change. And the start of that change is twofold: first is to admit that you're willing to change and that you need to change, while the second task is to take small immediate actions to start the process.

> *"No matter how short or long your journey to your accomplishment is, if you don't begin you can't get there. Beginning is difficult, but unavoidable!"*
>
> *- Israelmore Ayivor*

What do you want your future to be?

We talked about this earlier. If you had a crystal ball or a Genie in a bottle, what would you ask for? The first answer for most people, of course, is money.

I was fortunate enough a few years ago to have closed enough business that a single commission check, after taxes, was large enough to pay off the balance of my outstanding mortgage. I can not even begin to describe the feeling I got when I wrote the check to the mortgage company!

All of us dream of the day when we are able to retire, regardless of how we define retirement. The pertinent question is whether or not you have a plan to accumulate enough resources to fund the lifestyle of your dreams, in the timeframe you desire.

CONCLUSION

One of the many lessons of the 2020 COVID experience is that many professionals can perform their job remotely. Even to the extent that some have realized their dream of spending, as an example, a month skiing in Colorado in a rented house yet still working productively. They start and end the day with a run down the slopes.

Envision how your work environment would change with a newfound respect from your boss, your peers and management as you became a consistent achiever.

And all of these, and more, would contribute greatly to a less stress life. One where you could enjoy your family, your work, your free time more fully.

One of the benefits I realized when I was consistently in the top 10% of my peers was a freedom to pursue projects that interested me. Since I was able to achieve my annual quota in 9 months, I had the time to pursue these projects. Granted, they all had the potential to contribute increased revenue to the organization and more commission to me. Not only was the time important but because I was at my number, consistently, the organization was glad to provide resources.

Just imagine the feeling of waking up in the morning, every morning, eager to face and conquer the world!

And what if you do not act now?

It's really quite simple. Here's what it'll be like if you don't act now:

- If you're frustrated today, you'll just be more frustrated tomorrow.
- If you stressed now, you'll continue to be stressed.

- If you're short on money, you'll continue to be short on money.
- If you uncertain about your job prospects for the future, you'll just have to get used to that bad feeling.
- And if you feel guilty because you're not providing for your family as you'd like to, well you might as well accept that as your reality.

Things don't get better because we want them to. They only get better because we work to make them better.

Don't think about making lots of big changes. Focus on making one small change – NOW. And another small change tomorrow. And another small change the day after that. But start with the change now. It's not that hard and we're here to help you.

"The only impossible journey is the one you never begin."

- *Anthony Robbins*

Thanks for reading. I hope it was worth your time.

A FEW WORDS

On the Power of a Master Mind Group

Change is hard. Not necessarily because the steps are complex, but because we as humans have difficulty accepting things about ourselves.

> *"We become great, not by changing the world, but by loving the world and changing ourselves."*
>
> ***Debasish Mridha***

What is a Master Mind Group (MMG)

It's a **group** of your **peers** who **meet regularly** and **focus** on resolving a **specific problem** or set of problems. They could be business, social, community, or personal. They could be brainstorming sessions or have specific objectives and outcomes.

A mastermind group is **designed for the members** to learn and to **assist** the other members in learning.

It is a **safe environment** based on **trust and respect**.

MMGs have focus, objectives, agendas, and a facilitator. But they run on **participation and engagement**.

They provide **accountability**, in a non-threatening way.

They bring together potentially new and different **perspectives**, allowing all members to **gain insight** into their specific situations. Sometimes, we can understand our issues and the possible resolutions when they are presented in a **new light**.

> *If you want to go fast, go alone. If you want to go far, go together.*
>
> **— *African Proverb***

It can be very difficult to find a **safe, non-judgmental** sounding board for our questions and concerns. Friends and family often do not have the **objective perspective** we need. Business associates, especially in sales, could have **ulterior motives**. Many people will answer our questions from **their perspective** and not provide the insight we are seeking.

Many people will not share their concerns or allow others to help them if they are **not comfortable** with the group. These individuals will then not contribute causing the other members to hold back their involvement. This may occur without the members even realizing it.

There are benefits to joining a MMG. **Simply being** a member of a group with **aligned goals** and objectives can provide significant value.

There is no doubt that **creativity and innovation** are essential for business success in today's world. While nothing is actually "new", they may be to us as individuals. A business or individual can make improvements in their goals by **gaining new viewpoints** with the other members of the MMG.

As humans, we tend to **get caught in our own perspectives** and myopic in our thinking, **especially under stress**. Having new inputs can free us from ourselves and open new possibilities for us. **Honest feedback** can be empowering, especially when its combined with accountability.

Goals can be hard to keep. A recent study shows that a whopping **92% of people fail** to meet their goals. Yikes!

We all are prone to 'shiny object syndrome.' And having a peer group to keep you **accountable** is one of the best ways to move you into action!

A common outcome of MMGs is a **clearer perspective** and **renewed enthusiasm** about solving a problem or achieving a goal.

Just to be clear, let's define what a MMG is not. A MMG may have aspects and qualities of other types of help structures. There are differences. One is not better than the other. Each one has a **specific structure and purpose**.

The largest differentiator is the relationship of the members to each other and the role of the organizer or facilitator. In the MMG structure, all members are contributors and active participants. They create the discourse. They are not simply recipients.

The organizer in an MMG is a member of the group and acts as a facilitator, **gently guiding** the interactions.

Here are some alternative structures that **can be confused** with MMGs, but are not: a class, group coaching, a mentoring group, and a networking group.

Master Mind Groups can be **any size**. They can be three people; they can be 100 people. When you look at the intent though of a MMG, it becomes clear that groups in the range of five to ten members are probably the **most efficient**. The main determinant of group size is the intent or objective of the Master Mind. So, most issues are solved best with fewer members while others require a broader perspective.

How long does a MM stay connected? Much like the answer above, **it depends**. As a MMG is formed to achieve a **specific objective**, the real question becomes how long it **should take to achieve** that objective. For relatively straightforward problems, it could be two or three or four meetings. For others, the duration could be in weeks, months, or even years.

Here are the keys to a successful MMG

Purpose / focus / topic: What unites the group is a central issue or problem or question that all members are interested in addressing and resolving for themselves as well as the other members.

Facilitation: There needs to be an individual responsible to keep the group meetings on track. This is not the role of a manager but that of a coach or guide.

Commitment: Each member needs to be committed to the group, to the objectives, and to its success. Part of that commitment includes attending the meetings and being prepared.

Participation: The purpose of the mastermind is to share and to learn through that sharing. Thus, attending the meetings and not participating - listening and giving - really doesn't help the group or yourself

Follow the rules: They are not designed to hinder participation and learning but rather to simply ensure that housekeeping matters are understood. This ensures the best possible experience for all members.

Enthusiasm: Have you ever sat with somebody to discuss a topic and they were monotone, unengaged, stiff, and unresponsive? I bet you didn't have a whole lot of fun on that one! The purpose of the MMG is to help you achieve your goals and to help the other members do the same. Let's get enthusiastic about success!

Honesty: With yourself and others. Another way to express this is Vulnerability. One of the biggest benefits of the MMG is that it allows you a safe environment to express your issues and concerns and opinions. The quality of your experience in the group will be directly in proportion to your ability to be honest and accept honesty from others.

> *"When you surround yourself with positive people then you can learn, grow and build an empire because the quality of your life is determined by the quality of people you associate with."*
>
> — *Dhiraj Kumar Raj*

Dedicated to:

Dee
The Boys & Chin
RBL
Jimmy K

NEXT STEPS

Congratulations. You finished the book. I hope you found it worth your time and attention. And, Yes, I would like to know!

Now you might be wondering what to do next to empower yourself to live the life of your dreams. I can help, here's how:

For immediate and significant improvement in your Mindset and sales, become a member of an exclusive **MindSet Mastery for Sales Success MasterMind** at **www.AttitudeSelling.com**.

Join the Attitude Selling Facebook Group at

https://www.facebook.com/Attitude-Selling-110280607897337

Reach me at John.Lester@AttitudeSelling.com.

I hope to see you in the Winners Circle!

ACKNOWLEDGEMENTS

"My father said this to me: "Israelmore, if you don't make any impact on earth, you will die before you die. But if you impress hearts with what you do, you still live even after you are gone"

— *Israelmore Ayivor*

I believe it is right and proper to remember and give thanks for people who enter our lives and positively impact us. I have been very fortunate to have met a few of these. At the time, I did not always realize their impact, their generosity, and their contribution. And their humanity.

I want to take a moment here and say, "Thank You". Some can no longer hear these words, but I want to express them from my heart.

I can not list them all and will celebrate those that left, and continue to leave, the deepest impact on my life.

- Phil Sciara
- Brad Mack

- Mike Perez
- Jim Felicetti
- Steve Lance
- John von Sternberg
- Mike Stewart
- Aman Agarwal
- Eric Fenton
- **Smurf and Newk**
- **The Ostrich Posse**
- **Keenan**

ABOUT THE AUTHOR

I started my career as a computer repair technician and went to work for a small local distributor of a specialized desktop machine for Life Insurance Actuaries. As life takes its turns, my boss came into my office one sunny morning to inform me that our little organization had severed its ties with the manufacturer and that he did not need a technician if we didn't have sales. Not knowing what I didn't know, of course I agreed to take on the role of salesperson!

It took me a number of years fighting the fear of rejection, of not knowing where I was in the sales process and of not generating consistent sales and commissions before I enrolled in professional sales training. But even after that, and for years to follow, there was always a nagging feeling that something was missing.

As quoted by Sun Tzu in "the Art of War", "Victorious warriors win first and then go to war, while defeated warriors go to war first and then seek to win"

I have attended many sales training programs and classes and read numerous books on sales. They do not discuss the perspective and positioning necessary for successful selling. They do not focus on MindSet!

This shift in my perspective has allowed me to achieve multiple sales President Clubs for overachievement and numerous awards for performance. As well as afford to live in a very desirable community and volunteer for causes that inspire me.

Good hunting!

www.ingramcontent.com/pod-product-compliance
Lightning Source LLC
Chambersburg PA
CBHW052330220526
45472CB00001B/358